Grub Up

Explorer Challenge

Find out what minibeast
this bird meets ...

OXFORD
UNIVERSITY PRESS

Dad had cooked macaroni cheese for dinner.
"I loved this when I was a boy," he said.
He gave all the children a plate of macaroni.

The children pushed their plates away.
"We don't like macaroni cheese," said
Kipper.
"But you haven't even tasted it," said Dad.

"We don't like the look of it," said Kipper.
"That's all there is," said Dad, firmly. "So eat it up or go hungry."

"We didn't have a proper dinner," said Chip,
later. "I'm hungry. It's not fair."
Suddenly the key began to glow.

"We can't go on an adventure now," said Kipper. "We are still hungry. That's even more unfair."

The key took them to a hot, dry place. It was the outback in Australia.

"Why are we here?" asked Kipper. "It's just lots of trees and bushes."

"I think we are in the bush in Australia," said Chip.

"I wonder what that boy is doing?" said Biff.
"He seems to be picking something out of a hole."

"Honey ants! This is a lucky find,"
said the boy. "Tuck in. There are plenty
of them."

Each ant had a sac of honey on it.

"Yuk," said Kipper. "We can't eat ants."

"You don't eat them, just suck out the honey," said the boy.

"Er ... no, thank you," said Chip.

"You won't last long in the bush," said
the boy. "Insects are good bush tucker."
"Bush tucker?" asked Biff. "What is
bush tucker?"

"It's food that's all around us," said the boy. "In the bush, you have to eat what you can find."

The boy's name was Dalman.
"I am learning to hunt for food and find water," he said.

"Water is hard to find. The bush is a hot, dry place. Sometimes we can find water in little rock pools."

He dug into the roots of a tree and gently pulled out a grub.

"Fantastic!" he said. "Witchetty grubs. Try one. They are great bush tucker."

"Eat a wriggly grub?" said Biff. "No thanks."
"I don't fancy eating a grub," said Chip.

"It's time for me to go home," said Dalman.
"You need to eat bush tucker if you want to
survive in the bush."

Just then the key glowed. The adventure was over.

"Perhaps we were too fussy," said Chip.
"Let's find Dad and say sorry."

"And let's see if there is any macaroni cheese left," said Biff.

"This must be Dad's tucker," said Chip, with a grin.

"It's not bad," said Kipper. "But what does this tube of macaroni remind you of?"

Retell the Story

Look at the pictures and retell the story in your own words.

Look Back, Explorers

Can you name one of the insects Dalman suggested they eat?

What was Dalman learning in the bush?

The bush is decribed as a 'hot, dry place'. What other words can you think of to describe it?

Imagine you are in the bush with Dalman. What questions would you ask him?

Did you find out what minibeast this bird met?

What's Next, Explorers?

Now you have seen Biff, Chip and Kipper looking for minibeasts in the bush, find out about lots of amazing minibeasts ...

Minibeasts Matter!

Claire Llewellyn
Series created by Roderick Hunt and Alex Brychta

OXFORD

Explorer Challenge
for *Minibeasts Matter!*

Find out what this minibeast eats ...